This Walker book belongs to:

....

....

....

For Paul and Adam

First published 1988 by Walker Books Ltd
87 Vauxhall Walk, London SE11 5HJ

This edition published 2016

4 6 8 10 9 7 5 3

© 1988, 1998 Shirley Hughes

The right of Shirley Hughes to be identified as author/illustrator
of this work has been asserted by her in accordance with
the Copyright, Designs and Patents Act 1988

This book has been typeset in Plantin

Printed in China

British Library Cataloguing in Publication Data:
a catalogue record for this book is available
from the British Library

ISBN: 978-1-4063-7242-7

www.walker.co.uk

OUT AND ABOUT
A FIRST BOOK OF POEMS

Shirley Hughes

WALKER BOOKS
AND SUBSIDIARIES

LONDON · BOSTON · SYDNEY · AUCKLAND

A NOTE FROM SHIRLEY HUGHES

Poetry doesn't always have to rhyme, though it is sometimes
fun when it does. For me, words and pictures go together,
so I cannot think of an idea for a poem without sitting down
at my drawing board and searching for my paints.
Out and About is about being out there in all weathers,
and about the joy of wind, mud and snow, as well as the seaside
and playing outdoors on a sunny day.
Katie and her baby brother Olly are always ready to
open the back door and set out down the garden path to
see what each day has to offer.
This collection of poems gives a taste of what they might find
when they are out and about; small things like leaves or puddles,
or huge things like sky or a beach or a windy hill.
Some of the illustrations in this book have no words at all.
But I am hoping that perhaps some of my readers might feel like
making up poems of their own to go with them, inspired by
what *they* have seen when they were out and about.

Shirley Hughes

CONTENTS

SPRING

Out and About

Shiny boots,
Brand new,
Pale shoots
Poking through.
In the garden,
Out and about,
Run down the path,
Scamper and shout.
Wild white washing
Waves at the sky,
The birds are busy
And so am I.

Mudlarks

I like mud.
The slippy, sloppy, squelchy kind,

The slap-it-into-pies kind.

Stir it up in puddles,
Slither and slide.

I *do* like mud.

Spring Greens

Bulbs in pots,

Twigs in jars,

Dads in the street, washing cars.

Greens in season,

Trees in bud,

Sky in puddles,

Ripples in mud.

Birds in bushes, singing loud,

Sun tucked up in a bed of cloud.

Hill

Huge clouds
Slowly pass;
Huge hill
Made of grass.
Jungle under,
Thick and green,
Tangled stalks –
Creep between;
Scramble up,
Hug the ground...

Suddenly see
All around!
Watch out, fences,
Fields and town!
From the top of the world
I come rolling down.

Sunshine at Bedtime

Streets full of blossom,
Like pink and white snow,
Beds full of tulips,
Tucked up in a row.

Trees full of "candles"
Alight in the park,
Sunshine at bedtime,
Why isn't it dark?

Yet high in the sky
I saw the moon,
Pale as a ghost
In the afternoon.

SUMMER

Water

I like water.
The shallow, splashy, paddly kind,
The hold-on-tight-it's-deep kind.

Slosh it out of buckets,
Spray it all around.

I *do* like water.

Squirting Rainbows

Bare legs,
Bare toes,
Paddling pool,
Garden hose.
Daisies sprinkled
In the grass,
Dandelions
Bold as brass.
Squirting rainbows,
Sunbeam flashes,
Backyards full
Of shrieks and splashes!

Seaside

Sand in the sandwiches,
Sand in the tea,
Flat, wet sand running
Down to the sea.
Pools full of seaweed,
Shells and stones,
Damp bathing suits
And ice-cream cones.

Waves pouring in
To a sand-castle moat.
Mend the defences!
Now we're afloat!
Water's for splashing,
Sand is for play,
A day by the sea
Is the best kind of day.

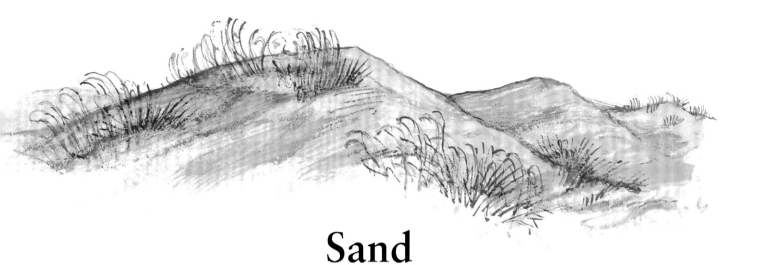

Sand

I like sand.
The run-between-your-fingers kind,
The build-it-into-castles kind.
Mountains of sand meeting the sky,
Flat sand, going on for ever,
I *do* like sand.

The Grass House

The grass house
Is my private place.
Nobody can see me
In the grass house.
Feathery plumes
Meet over my head.
Down here,
In the green, there are:
Seeds
Weeds
Stalks
Pods
And tiny little flowers.

Only the cat
And some busy, hurrying ants
Know where my grass house is.

AUTUMN

Feasts

Apples heaped on market barrows,
Juicy plums and stripy marrows.

Grains of barley,
Carefully stored,

Feasts of berries,

Nuts to hoard,

And ripe pumpkins, yellow and green,
To light with candles at Hallowe'en.

Wind

I like the wind.
The soft, summery, gentle kind,
The gusty, blustery, fierce kind.
Ballooning out the curtains,
Blowing things about,
Wild and wilful everywhere.
I *do* like the wind.

Wet

Dark clouds,
Rain again,
Rivers on the
Misted pane.
Wet umbrellas
In the street,
Running noses,
Damp feet.

Misty

Mist in the morning,
Raw and nippy,
Leaves on the pavement,
Wet and slippy.
Sun on fire
Behind the trees,
Muddy boots,
Muddy knees.

Shop windows,
Lighted early,
Soaking grass,
Dewy, pearly.
Red, lemon,
Orange and brown,
Silently, softly,
The leaves float down.

WINTER

44

Sick

Hot, cross, aching head,
Prickly, tickly, itchy bed.
Piles of books and toys and puzzles
Heavy on my feet,
Pillows thrown all anyhow,
Wrinkles in the sheet.
Sick of medicine, lemonade,
Soup spooned from a cup.
When will I be *better*?
When can I *get up*?

Fire

Fire is a dragon
(Better beware),
Dangerous and beautiful
(Better take care).
Puffing out smoke
As soon as it's lit,
Licking up leaves,
Crackle and spit!

Sending up sparks
Into the sky
That hover a moment
And suddenly die.
Fire is a dragon,
Alive in the night;
Fiery dragon,
Glittering bright.

Cold

Cold fingers,
Cold toes,
Pink sky,
Pink nose.
Hard ground,
Bare trees,
Branches crack,
Puddles freeze.
Frost white,
Sun red,
Warm room,
Warm bed.

Hoping

Grey day,
Dark at four,
Hurry home,
Shut the door.
Think of a time
When there will be
Decorations
On a tree,
Tangerines,
And hot mince pies,
A bulging stocking,
A Christmas surprise!

ABOUT THE AUTHOR

Shirley Hughes has illustrated more than
200 children's books and is one of the
best-loved writers for children.
She has won the Kate Greenaway Medal
twice and has been awarded an OBE for her
distinguished service to children's literature.
In 2007, *Dogger* was voted the UK's
favourite Kate Greenaway Medal-winning
book of all time.

More classic picture books by
SHIRLEY HUGHES:

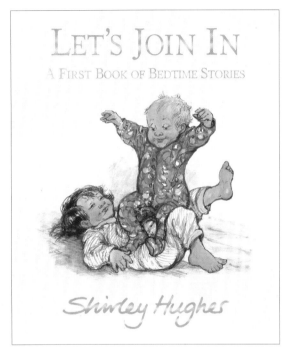

ISBN 978-1-4063-6440-8

ISBN 978-1-4063-6097-4

"One of our best-loved children's writers and illustrators."
Daily Mail

"No one can match Shirley Hughes in the simple mastery of both words and pictures."
Times Educational Supplement

Available from all good bookstores

www.walker.co.uk